The call of the ink bird

Laura Demelza Bosma

ISBN-13: 978-0995358157

ISBN-10: 099535815X

The Call Of The Ink Bird by/
Laura Demelza Bosma

Cover image and internal images by Laura Demelza Bosma
www.laurademelzabosma.com
Author Photo by Igor Corbeau

Tandava Press
www.tandavapress.com
tandavapress@gmail.com

Printed in The United States of America on plantation stock

For My Beloved Heath

Drunk on poetry, love, poetry, love...

Want some more?

Impregnate with satisfaction.

Yes, more, more.

Contents

The Call Of The Ink Bird

Thus The Whales Fly

The writer's introduction to 'Call of the ink bird'

Thank you for picking up this book. I am happy to welcome you into the landscapes of my own personal reality and imagination. I am deeply thankful for getting this opportunity to share my poetry, my inner spark that I want to bring into the world on paper again! It is already ten years ago that my first poetry chapbook got published in my mother language Dutch, by a Dutch Publisher. A lot has happened since: I've lived poetry for a while until I thought I'd lost it because of moving country and not having a poetry-world to dwell in anymore. I became a mother and a single mother. When I felt alone in the dark it was poetry who came to pick me up and take me home. I did not move back to my poetry-world in Holland but I did move back to the centre of my love and joy, where the poetry arises. I am convinced of it now, once you drank from the inner well of creativity, you have to get back there and you will.

I want to tell you something about the build-up of this book. When I took a closer look at the poems to decide in which order they had to appear, I recognized that there were four types of poem to be found, looking at their subjects.

1. Poems about pregnancy and new life.
2. Poems about blossoming, in the middle of life.

3. Poems about decay.

4. Poems about (light in the) darkness.

In the poems I am looking through a young woman's eyes, my own eyes but also the eyes of the universal woman. It seems there is an old woman speaking sometimes with the voice of a girl and when the young girl speaks the wisdom of the old woman comes through. She observes from her centre as the seasons pass through her, the season of new life, the season of motherhood, through the decay, into darkness. I wanted to call her 'Deciduous Woman,' because like the tree she stands in her middle and watches while she feels her leaves grow, while she carries apples to let them go when ripe, while her leaves flame up before they lose colour and fall, while she is naked and gets covered in a white coat of cold.

How did the birds get in?

To each of the four parts I wanted to make an illustration. I have not been thinking about birds, but the same way as their presence arose naturally in the poems, they also appeared 'out of the blue' into my drawings. I wanted to paint all around the subject of the tree-woman, but it just didn't feel right until a bird came in. The birds made me feel in love with the creative process itself, and as an artist this is the ultimate feeling: the road as destination.

My poems often contain a sadness or even a darkness about them, but also while writing them I have been feeling 'the bird.' They were 'now' as could be for me, they appeared and they allowed me to grab their spirit into a poem.

Mainly since the pregnancy of my daughter in 2010 I have dreams wherein animals appear to deliver me messages without words. Generally, these dreams make me feel 'in awe' and I wake up speechless and energized.

In Austrian-German the people say about someone who is seen as crazy that this person has a bird (in their head). I have been blamed for having a bird! Yes, I have a bird, we each 'have' all birds and also all the other lifeforms exist within us, because we are one and the same. Imagine a bird having a human, this would be at least as crazy as the other way around. Animal-dreams come to me with such an intensity that I know what is right, where I have to go.

The four birds that wanted to show up as an illustration are, in order of appearance:

1. Wren. (spring 2015 my loved one gave me a new life of hope and introduced the wren to me, views of forests appeared again, even inside.)

2. Kingfisher. (For no explainable reason this bird reminds me of a summer of dreams turning into flesh. In a mixture of imagination and reality there was a blue house, an island and his guitar. A love-epos that shaped my artist's heart and my singing voice.)

3. Owl (autumn 2015 a real owl looked into my eyes while I was driving home. A few weeks before this event I had first met the owl on a shamanic journey. Also, the owl is my mother's favourite animal.)

4. Swan. (winter 2011 I have been mourning over a dead swan who was part of a couple that I often admired, when I was in emotional pain another winter, the swan came to me in the poem 'The Swan's Shen.' Shen means as much as 'spirit' in various Chinese religions.)

The same way I wish for the poems, I also want the four illustrations to speak for themselves. To the one illustration on the cover though, I want to share with you the story of it's becoming.

As a baby, toddler and small child my parents often took me for a walk to the park. In the park there was what seemed a special little palace for the peacock. I thought of him as magic.

In my twenties I had a spiritual dream about what I called 'the Lord of the peacock.' There was a loving man in the peacock's palace of my youth and there were other spirit's celebrating with him. I was a girl, going into the park, walking to a little stream where I sang my song. The song combined with the water of the stream turned into a flower, like some secret alchemistic brew. I took the flower back to the Lord and felt intense happiness when he received my flower with a loving smile and I woke up.

Later, through the practice of Hatha Yoga I felt attracted to mantra-singing which caused me to visit the ashram Sadha Shiva Dham in Loenen, The Netherlands. The Guru I loved and admired was Shiva, the lord of the peacock. I saw the bright pictures of Shiva and the peacock and was reminded of my memories. Somehow the call of the peacock brought me in touch with the spark of my creativity, as did the mantras. Funny enough, the press this little book got printed by is called Tandava Press, revering to the dancing Shiva!

I did the four other illustrations before considering the theme of the cover. Because of moving place I was sorting our my box with drawings and my lover's eye fell upon a colourful one of a fantasy-peacock, the only one I ever drew. He absolutely loved him and because of his enthusiasm I got to the idea to use the peacock for the cover. I've been mentioning Ink-birds here at home and here my love recognized one, it's the ink-bird, the call of the ink bird! Because the style of the drawing did not fully fit the other ones I made a new one.

We have decided to add my translations from my first Dutch poetry chapbook *'Thus the whales fly'* to this book, so you can see where I have come from poetically but also spiritually. Where the darkness surrounded my light, I now know how to be light, giving space to the darkness.

I hope this book helps you, at least a bit, to find home in yourself and hear your own calling.

With love,

Laura

I Paint Forests On Our Wall

So You Can Fly

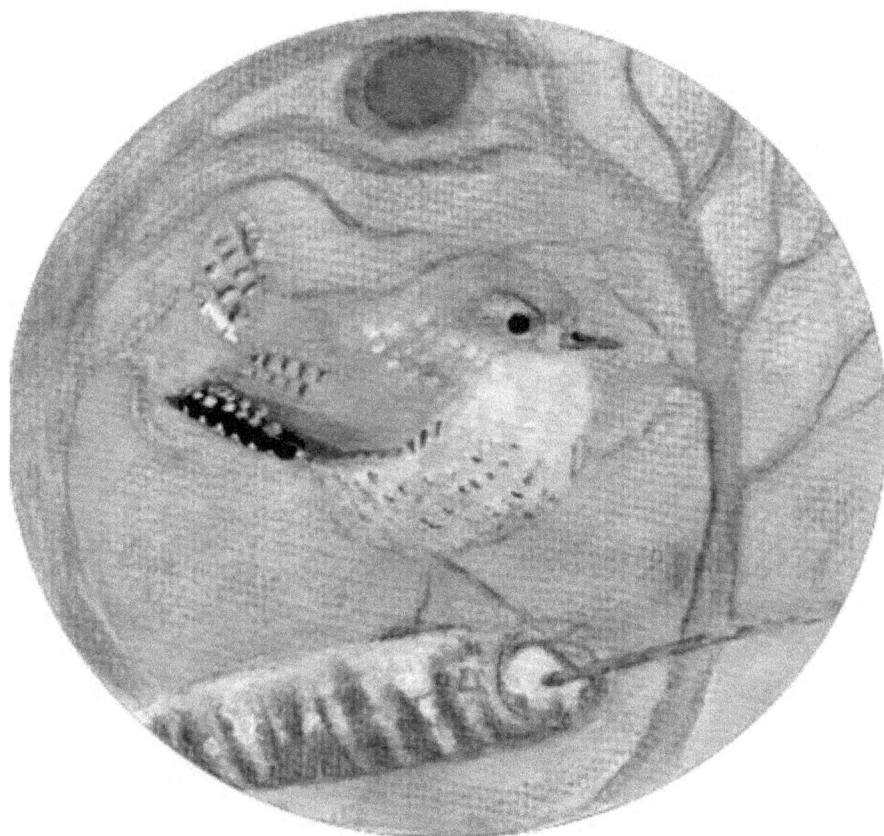

Chrystall painter

The pencils I want to draw the world with
I stick in my hair, there are two:
a black and a white, yet they maintain all colours.

The same way the mountain holds life
in her rocky fist. Pure emerald
emerges in fluid streams when I open my hips
which are my granddaughter's hips,
Persephone's hips. My past unfolding
rolls like a spiralling carrousel from
where I stand now into the dark space.

Filled with wonder
the ends of my hair
glow to paint with.

Out of the book into the stream

I open the book and you start reading
and while reading I feel I am the female part of you.
I sit down on a stone besides the stream
and witness how your guiding voice is taken over by the water.
The book floats downstream until it's gone.

We move there where we can be more,
where our feet bring us. We move into
heartbeat-driven and wide-eyed witnessing the beauty of us.
Our four feet together step into the cold so we feel the tingle.

You carry me as I sing.
This way we demand to be taken
by the living story of a stream.

There we go into here.
No one speaks but the forest is vibrant.
All her eyes, songs, hearts, leaves,
love about us.

Goddess birthing music

Where I am tired the garden revitalizes me with her soft paws,
welcomes me with her touch on animals' pathways.
Miss tarantula opening Eden for mammals.

To surround life, the same way life is surrounding me
my steps softly draw the shape of love's pregnant body.

Soon I'm about to turn the inner music inside out.
With lungs gasping the butterfly will open up fresh wings.
Here, around earth, where longing and air exist to float on.

I imagine this, then turn back to what is.
Rhythms pulsing without my interfering.

The primal woman with cow horn-earrings carrying
water uphill wiggles her hips on stillness's deep beat.

Birthing music is the blood-flower's expression.

Snow-white's courage

Seven-league boots don't suit anyone.
Imagine Snow-white stamped away with them.
To where, she asks. She would have to go
to the highest mountain from the whole of
Laniakea to oversee it all from her beauty.

No, the thorns had to go in these feet.
The hunter had to be driven to the edge of his knife
to surrender himself, sobbing in smithereens.
A boy for her life suddenly, the raw leather
a ridiculous costume.

And where would have been the hilarious fever in dwarf skulls?
If some magic would have given seven-league boots to this girl?
And where for her the charm of being stranded at the feet of seven men,
one-by-one too small to be true, in a hole black enough to start
hallucinating?

There passes the witch, deadly beautiful from being tired.
Blood-alone with her orders. Through her mirror-daughter
she learns what poison cannot bite away. Step or not,
she's someone's beloved.

But sometimes one creature is made to poison another
and the boots that exist, to rapidly get away

are only valid in another tale, in an adjacent cluster.

She can never leave from what wants to die or emerge from her.

There passes a prince with a blind karma.

He can't do anything else.

That kiss is another 'Oh this moment.'

To live now is the new happily ever after.

Little wren

For my three children

You are a little wren.
Can you send yourself
on the breath of the wind
overseas?

Yes, my heart is inside the world
that's where you open me up.
I paint forests on our wall
so you can fly

in our room. That's where
the sun comes up.

The daughter unformed

Life needs to pull a woman's hair from behind
on the slide down, saying 'mother, mother.'
She looks back into the soul's eye, into love is a thriller.
Some bloodcurdling vortex where copies of yourself
get born to use your every drop of colour.

Yes to flesh but not yet. Raving with physical love,
sweat, hair-growth, body-boat to body-boat.
Taken by the sea, raving on a beat.
Yes, yes but not yet…
As soon as you get there the daughter's spell
will slip into your hunger.

The mother slowly brushing her hair
static into heaven.
The soul drinks from her stillness.

Where a mother-to-be softens herself
the sound of every breaking hair
is a poem.

The daughter's space

She is in my centre, clings herself into red earth's body,
drinks the forest in through the cord, the leaves' song
of oxygen, gathers strength with the natural turning
of the wheel.

The daughter stepped into her own absence.
The open space where I held my breath
when the crow screamed before it left.

My virgin's feet drawn to the middle
of where my sister got burned,
island of life in the ocean of death.
I catch my womanhood and her soul like a flame.

Emptiness recites for me, the mother concept.
The beating fever of life finds her home
whether or not I am.

Leboyer*

Captain Birth dictates to be on the top of each wave,
to stay awake, to not be swept away but be swept through,
to stay true to the tone that is you, to be on that tone,
he dictates, Mister Lighthouse, her glowing shorelines
floating on focus.

He guides her with a choir of bees.
He guides her with the tambura and the no-sound of
peace, from deep out of the earth, vibrating through sea.

With the strictness rooted in love of a born teacher
he does the only thing he can do, opening mermaids
tails into legs, cervixes melting open for babies
as they happen, naturally.

* Frédérick Leboyer (1/11/1918 - 25/5/2017) was a French obstetrician
and author, best known for his 1975 book, *Birth Without Violence*, which
popularized gentle birthing techniques.

The trap of life's song

Dedicated to Kate Bush

You get me, in your trap of a song,
get me caught up in the landscape
I call forever mine.

The touch of your song sensualizes my body
and I wander through it since

every day
it's sound gives birth to me anew
and to you in me
and to me in you
and out of ourselves:

a home that breathes
a home that changes shape
with how we move through her.

This is the only adventure I call thrilling
and at the same time forever safe.
My hands and my little ones' can't help but
paint whatever faints already in its coming to life.

All is made out of tone, light-,
bodies.

Boy-shaped mudra

For Davin Salomon

In a puddle in a dream
I am considering reality.
With my feet I touch
earth mixed with water.
My mother's face
is a moving imprint in clay.

She who gives me my boots
and the truth.
Every moment of everyday
she moves as I do
here, in standing still.

I observe the fire-dragon
in my chest. My breath
a dangling paper-bird.
Watching my stillness,
my being like a stone,
my two fists.

I see life
where the sun reflects
I might get dirty.

The boy's Li

Li from Lion and Taoist Li
from living long haired
open hearted for the world
a little curl in the neck
a spontaneous wildlife-swirl

A life force that sweats itself away
from under the blanket
into the room with no roof

Li stretching into the branches
into trees, dreams of the woods

What he sees when he first looks
is what he cuts out, is what he
calls to life with one yell, LI.

The faces of creation

Voluminous mother tree, you've done well.
In the rage of unstoppable creation.
When the sky broke open inside of your centre.
When the wind of change tore off your sweet masks.

You, skeleton with a beating heart. 'Well' is what
always is, even when you miss, when you skip
a beat. When you feel like your child: in need.

In the bay, you are the bay. You are That,
eternally wide, holding space for no-self.
Expression through the faces of creation.

Eye-landscape

We go out in the child's eye that just woke.
We go out in the awakened eye.
It's brightness makes it hard to recognize
whether we are fine or drowning.

There seems to be no border here between this
and the other side, no time before
the first gasping for breath.

You take me into something
of this universe of timelessness.
Into the clear pond of our eye,
life's child.

If There Is Only This One Island, We Should Live Here

The butterfly of revolution

I am on the hill watching the big-boned woods
through the clear glasses of my blank mind.
Nature appears sharp, the sky-scratchers faint.
I am calm as rice is white, this way it is right.

Mammoth-trees filter the toxicity out of the air.
My day-dream comes with the same clarity as the view.
A girl calling herself the Butterfly with the vision
to filter the toxicity out of the human race
clings herself to a redwood-tree. Wondering:

What if I have to come down
to find out the kids still lay paralyzed,
in the dead-ends of labyrinths they find in their phones?
If nothing changed after all my breath of revolution
went through the poisonous system?

Now, has the possibility of a healed earth collapsed
like social media suggests? Is it true the people
remained unconscious, for the soft beauty
of her tender eyes on wings for nature?

Years after her come-down
on a hill, overlooking the trees I grasp
the butterfly of revolution effortlessly into my chest
without damaging her flight of colour.

Two-headed dragon

For Rémi Sylvan Benjamin

You lead me back to the land of calm between branches,
naming the unnameable with me.

Ordering a tree-house we end up in a shed
with a window sized half the roof,
so filthy though we can't see through.

We find each other's eyes as clearer reflections of the forest inside.
I can tell by the amount of oxygen when I breathe you in,
you are the lover of my laughter.

This is our son. What we thought to be impossible materialized
in the midst of insects, parties, sunburn:
our river-boy, our cooling sanctuary.

All we need is a bed in the forest where we can sleep and wake
whenever our body requests to be full of zest

for our love, books
and our son:

We are the two headed dragon
for its master Chan.

Whole lilies like suns above the theatre

Before him she has only been written on paper
and he is the saviour who is taking her out.
He sees a sprout of beauty at the height of her hips.
Says it's her daughter looking out of her future mist.
Says you are already in the blue shadow of her grip.
A ballerina in her music box driven by moonlight.

Theatre is just the same old lucid dream birds play.
The lilies floating in the pond
and the songs they catch from beyond.
Actors catching codes from an emblazoned
heavenly body. Flying mammals

looking whole about the illusion
that got torn into pieces
is what the director calls Metamorphosis.

In the face of the moon, the blood red director

We practise the poetess's words into a play:
Eating meat feels like eating myself.

'Lick her ear while you speak those words,'
the director says. 'I might understand
you better when you do.'

I watch the night fall on the other side
of the window, the sounds and the smells
of life are outside. There is a chamber
filled with trees in my chest of earth.

Demi-sexual in a row of voluptuous sister-bodies
I am unable to drive where another car is driving.
He who wants me to eat my sister,

brings me to the sea of my poetry-tears
in the glimmering silver of disassociation.

Saw Marc Chagall

Saw Marc Chagall in his element in Austria.
His house in the magic valley painted with
visions of people in their element, a woman
and her harp, a man and his straw hat,
his tiny wild garden encircled with Tibetan flags.

My little son pointed at a red helicopter
and saw the same. Everything and everyone
in the right element, all wearing different
eyes for what is beauty.

Love's fragrance is red

One dwarf says hello.

A friendly smile, the Geisha bows:

poppyflowerwave.

Lovewound

Tenderly designing, guiding
where the ivy has to grow up the wall
I draw the road of love
with lipstickleaves up the stairs
leading you to the fall in our bed

Where I am whole in bits
my youth leaks through my fingers
while the children jump on the couch
we will leave the one with the warwounds
in the old house, a new one
awaits us with more comfort

Veils of red lips, the humming silence
presses beneath the screams of a wildness
that I can not raise
a scratch bites in my blood
that I can not tame

red in the shape of an animal, slowly
dries and turns into my skin again

Crimson apples

Get goats and build their home yourself
and I will fall in love.
In the daylight it looks like
it has been like this forever.

Look inside, how still the apples in their bowl.
Where there is no wind I can imagine
it takes just one moment and we're old.

Outside you are always this young bloke.
I would never ask to get that colour
off your cheeks.

Something naked to eat

Inside of my bitter coat goes Ms. Honey undercover.
Everywhere I go the landscape has a hunger.
There are no trees. The no reason lightning
from no Mr. Thunder could happen in a moment
and burn me six feet under.

No lover only others, in their bitter coats.
To spot a smile is to see a lifeboat.
A smile with teeth has a piano on board
for Ms. Honey to pop out for a song or two.
Bitter is just a pit in the mouth,
easy to spit out.

The earth wants our imprint and hers
on our black sheet coats and suits.

The landscape has a hunger
for nakedness and summer.

The scream in the dream

To wade through a mudflat of jellyfish skin
and a sea of yoghurt, looking for a hole
to fall in, is a curious thing to do.

To look for a hollow spine,
the dream-variation on the spiral staircase,
Where I can sing a song in my fall
that I normally do not dare to sing.
I only have to turn my eyes around, to fly.

Almost invisible still, I end up at the house door
with inside of my ribcage the three men,
that I grabbed in my fall.

I will sit at the kitchen table like before.
A porcelain geisha in a light t-shirt
with the ultrasound of my ribs on it.

Inside of me the primal scream lives free.

My outside asks:
'Would you like tea, mother?'

Moonfruit's dress

White as a piece of moonfruit,
head like a fallen apple
and the sea licking my toes.

Yes, I´ve got feet down there, not a tail.
Should I still hesitate to sing, afraid to be a siren
leading sailors astray from the real lighthouse,
my face in the sand dark as death?

No, moonfruit is a wafer-thin dress of innocence
to wear on the inside
for a child crying for depth.
Where an army of organs loves for love
on a beat so tranquilizing,
it is for us inside of me.

I save my heart, on the boat
on the stream of that blood,
marrying life. With two tender
wrists outstretched I claim:

Don´t catch me.
Don´t write words where it´s white

I stood up.
I´m digging a home for coming winter.
I am now.

Honey for the queen

On this day slow enough to hear flower-bulbs opening
I have convinced all the honeybees
that it is for the better to leave me on my own.
Yet, wherever I go I am reminded
of honeycomb sweetness as my home.

I think about how I can hear their buzzing
so much better now I am all alone,
That, in whatever kind of form
nature's expressions are love songs.

My body a curved pen
leaking honey for a poem
over the landscape,
into open minds.

Than the delicatessen of silence:
a white swan gliding by without want.
This moon comes up for me,
with cheeks endlessly cold and serene.

I take our petrified foetus into my grave

For J.

Being the misfits, we were on eternal holiday.
'In love,' I wrote in saliva on our rock.

You lived two weeks long in your complicated baseline
while I played: woman on some days,
on others cave, cold and hollow, open for echoes;
on water-days, I saved the words that we spoke in my blood.

Bathing slowly in myself
as if I was born under the sign of snail,
my breasts floated upwards to face the moon.
An apple's white inside was my skin for you to bite into.
The owl hooted as soon we became one.

The liquid of our creativity turned into a lake.
The water was falling from the rocks with the moves we made.
There were faces in the stones that met us with a seriousness
in their wrinkled expressions when we first opened up our eyes
after the beginning left us overwhelmingly drenched.

I wished the earth had opened her mouth
just to let us in and hold us,
just for our frail love to grow thick bones.
You would have got one of our heart chambers
to play all your instruments around your baseline.

The other chamber would have been for me,

to recite poetry around our love.

Now the owl hoots, everywhere I am not with you.

You play in one world.

I recite in another:

to no one but our petrified foetus a mother.

She thanks the universe for her

I love my soul for using her voice.
How easy can life be, to just let me love her for that!
For ages we could live inside of a shell
curled up like yin and yang.

She doesn´t need to do anything.
I just follow what I call
`The Geisha´s red fragrance.´
She is where the sweetness peaks,
slowly moving between the books.
She sleeps inside of them
with these cheeks to bite in.

Sometimes I stand beside her while she sleeps.
To wave away the kingfishers in awe
with the letters I write her.
My dilemma is :I love their colour in her dreams
but don´t want them to wake her up.

I see her doing everything.
I just see her for that!
How easy can life be watching a little robin
hopping from leaf to leaf...?
How faithful is she
kissing my soul with the red of a robin´s chest

every time she flies into my stillness?

If there is only this one island we should live there

if here is the spark, the medicine for the dying breed

of poems, here we should build our house.

I´ve got lungs with enough air to love her as long as

my heart beats.

Through her I am love, through her I know everything

about flying up, about finding a star in the thick blanket of night.

Everything is all right, my universe.

I love you.

In empty space, white raven-shaped, our poetry, our love

Maybe I wished for you because I did not believe
I could really meet you.

Sitting at my windowsill I called you, appreciator of my soul
I painted around you on the window, like a child
with breath and fingers.

Empty space white raven shaped.
Watched it evaporate,
moved on with the day,
forgot.

At night you enter my dreams bewitched.
Now I see you I recognize you, drinking from my bottle post poetry,
found on the shores of your yearning heart, where we are one.
Drunk on our private party where no one else exists.

Drunk on poetry, love, poetry, love…
Want some more?
Impregnate with satisfaction.

Yes, more, more.

Breathing a blush

For Livia Mimouna

The day comes as it is,

lays its light upon her body still asleep.

Her breaths rise in the landscape.

An invisible hand brings movement in the stillness.

Comes with the wind, blows through the wooden chimes,

hanging between our everyday home

and the other side of the French doors to Eden.

She moves, daylight inside of her.

It's one of those fragments a mother wants to capture.

Only a few weeks a year the fruit is ripe,

here where we are living.

The apple trees scent and your laughter enough to fulfil us.

My Complexions Of Orange

Fractal leaf

A leaf is a tree
a love poem free from body
light, sweet and perfect.

Finding home in nature

Again my thoughts were beautiful
but nature knew better and took me over.
Wherever I go her fingers stretch out in branches,
grass blades and thorns of brambles.

I feel how much she wants to take me into her,
hold me tight, surround me, until I turn into her
precious soil. But she waits.

Like a predator with a soul who knows
when it is time for which pray.

Will my soul fly up or shall my dreams
with my body just turn into soil completely?

I strangely enough find comfort in the thought
to stretch out my fingers in branches, grass blades,
thorns and a few seasons of blackberries.

Deciduous woman

When the heating falls out her bones moan.
As she loses sap her bark crinkles.
Her leaves colour a grandmother's witches-dress.
Her brew of a few drops is drank and given back
in the hooting of owls. Her heat felt by wolf-children
at her roots

For each spirit there is a chamber in which oneness is included
surrounded by the uniqueness of individual sparks.
Painted flames before killed by individual snuffers.
Just a girl might think the smith is a drunkard.

Chewing on liquorice in the city she loves you.
You are in her embrace while she leaves you.

A small branch cracking off.
Some dry rags of witches-dress
in loss of colour still adorn you.

The dentist's universe

I am a decanter in the shape of a woman.
The water is the same water
as is given to the whales as ocean,
wincing with life.

I am in the treatment room of the dentist.
Children point to the moonfish in my belly
I am the moonfish in my belly,
am the children.
The dead tooth of the mother.
The dentist filing it away.

Roots go deep into the gums like oceanic corals.
On the x-ray her skull lovably smiles a tunnel to palate.

There they fly:
angels, microscopically small.

Cat face

When everyone bought everything new
she escaped to the ruins of who bought everything new years ago.
Something ancient lies in her fresh eyes and smile,
in her light steps causing the castle to crunch.

She is a doula, not for a child to be born
but to soften up the way the past blackens
in everyone's face with her presence.
The slinky beauty holds her cat between us and herself
when a brand new camera arises and hisses:

'Life is a shadow theatre my love.
Let's dress our light in fancier
layers of shadow.'

The sea caught a train

She who left a chamber and it's piano,
her could have been piano for life,
her possible recycled coffin.
Keys falling out with the years,
teeth loosening up from the gum,
a visit of the tuner her adventure.

She who couldn't tame her wild snake
curls through circumstances with indifference.
He fills his hunger in her backpack, biting holes in her
favourite pieces. He sneaks out to drink her tears
and smiles (as far as snakes can smile),
catching her salty mice.

She,
is alive.

The caecum of tears is always left behind.
That's me she thinks.
The sea is a pretty free woman.

Sylvia

Dedicated to Sylvia Plath

Half woman, half shadow:
she writes a cake,
she bakes a dress,
she wears a book.

She is her cake, her dress, her book,
success or failure, in whole or in pieces.

She wears oven-gloves to not burn herself/
she doesn't wear oven-gloves so she burns herself.

She bites through the pain. No scream.
In silence a scar shoots into her depth.

Her son weaves a web for a chestnut
with toothpick legs and drawn eyes
for later behind the window,
for when mama opens up
to live some kind of life:

moving back and forth when the wind blows.

Universal foxy housewife

Swans are daughters. Husbands animal activists
coming home to wives who are just wives
to wash the blood away and hide the swans
so they can stay white in a mirror-pond
in a tower chamber.

Wives cry to sob the floor of their life.
It's their best kept secret way
to be the fluid moving universe.
A star, a saffron corn of rice

Thankful men can still be passionate about foxes.
Dear lover, please save my complexions of orange.

40

The cobwebs are the walls pubes,
whispers from the natural woman.
The unfolding wound I live in today
is named Sunday, mirroring
the day I got born in too early.

I am here in the wound with the couch
staring at the carpet that fits
with a cup of tea in my fist
to match with the heat of my smothering spirit.

The sun at her brightest and everyone quiet.
Only the lips of the muse move to spell
'Live' as my name.

Now burn me a book and write me a tree.
Dream the outside, around this shoebox.
The inner child is awake.

Vegetable island

Marimba for the dance of his fingers.
The shadow of tomorrow falls over us,
a melody amongst the blooming willow,
a bleeding from our romping minds.
The evening falls cool enough
to caress ourselves young again.

They say that somewhere in the world
a predator falls on another
when ex-lovers in loving
relive their halving.

Two open hearts,
surrounded by nothing.
Sleeping vegetarians
in one head of chicory.

You go as you arise

You disappeared again.
In a dream you died.
I did not stop you.
It was nice to see.

Your body was not there
and what I saw ascending
could not be called human anymore.

A singing ball with green light in it.
Even this shapeless you reminded me
of all the love in the world. Our meetings
are only about how to disappear from each other.

Why do we die, asks a child? Never
when we just keep on singing.

I found you again on Google Maps.
If dreams wherein we perish immortalize,
this is not too bad.

Chestnut-man in blue

For J.

There is this blue room in a life of mine
where I will get you back.

At a beach I find a heart-shaped treasure coated in shells.
There is nothing in it but red velvet,
scarlet of young blood from children's knees,
the colour of theatre's present lips-
not of something salty that lasts for long,
not the ocean's blueness to preserve us.

But I will find you back one or more births away,
a few chambers back or forwards.
When I had you in my now,
I glowed with cold eternity around me
but waves never had arms nor hands to hold us.

Once I almost found you back;
it was in a book about a girl who couldn't find God.
You played the jazz of her eyes and loved her
in a hut with a blue inside between two chestnut-trees.

Between this book's lines I tried to hide
and whisper until my favourite man
with chestnut leaf-sized hands
would wake up here, besides me.

Are you still near after I drank bottles of languages?
Now, that I cannot speak one like my own?

Inside of me lives this volcano of our love,
my nearest inner islands drift
in its blue warm bath.

I am the melody that lives
on your rhythm through the earth.

The invisible kiss

If you´re tired, just go to sleep,
if you´re happy don´t make your soul weep
over empty images. Stop drowning.

Each dog left alone will start howling if no one hears.
Let it howl to calm down.
Allow the dog the self-experience of howling.
It´s sound just as much a flight
as the dive of an owl.

The old owl lands on my shoulder,
she is the mother reading books aloud
teaching the magic happens
if the listener is gentle
and the storyteller's voice has wings
and this in on.
Through time and space
the roles are ever-changing.

We are only looking for the invisible
the no-me
the sea of light
the laughing after the fight
the brightness of some thoughtless being in the sun.

Come along, in this no-words
we kiss the answer.

Ancestor's breeze

Sitting at what once was a window
in what once was a castle
a soft breeze blows through my head.

Through what once will be empty skull
where once were thoughts,
where my senses form now a view of love,
of changing seasons and landscape.

I'm a quiet ancestor
flowering through body,
opening up.

In mandala

Even those who could not think in words thought
she had watched too many Tim Burton movies
when she body-painted her own skeleton
on her skin and slammed the door
to the world with a bang.

It must be a joke, she thought
that even the smallest
can be divided through the infinite.
Since this knowledge
nothing small can be called cute anymore.

In a kaleidoscope an alien
finds her left eye
to be the most beautiful star.
In the middle of a mandala without borders
she gets closed in by infinity.

Better shut the door
despite the draft,
better get lost inwards.

The Swan's Rarely Heard Ga-Oh

White is the landscape of loved and lost

She who hides in her branches in the black and white movie.

The black and white movie wherein no one talks.

No one talks where the hands are constantly expressing in motion.

In motion there is always the stillness in the background.

In the background I keep you with me.

The me who speaks does not know who she is.

Who she is, got lost in the octopus expressing with too many arms.

Too many arms to mime her own blackness.

Her own blackness of thoughts where the background is white.

The song of the white bear

His love shows up tonight in dark indigo.
The way the darkness makes stars
more visible as light he lies around me.

The black den around
the white bear.

But if he´s a piece of rock
we change the roles.
I cover him as snow.

I don´t make fire and I do not celebrate.
Just thinking about this black and white
accomplishing each other
is my third eye's beloved pine tree.

Where being is found
in two-sided reaching
the present roars.

Cliff of beauty

Know we will end up in the embrace of it all
the misunderstanding that surrounds us
is surrounded by deep understanding.

When we end as an I
we know we are not only
in the embrace of all
we also know
we are this embrace.

Like the layers of a rose
I never left a single you
and you never left
a single part of me.

In this composition
we move through colours
we do we do
we move
through fractals of petals

Following veins, we call our own
here on this cliff of beauty I sit
just to write this poem.

Strong cold heart

Not in your cabinet, never painted on porcelain.
More like a moss carpet in the forest
open for the theatre of light.

More spontaneous yet still.
More like a love-affair.
Never printed in a book.
Never supported.
More like support in itself,
like soup is soup in itself.
A nutritive planet in the universe's mouth

A God doesn't taste, He just stirs and stirs
in the same cycle, more like amazed
while He never wonders.

Whale fishes wanted by the blue-lipped kiss
of two immense cold-hearted oceans as one.

There, unnoticed by the wandering of plastic
bags and nets from polluted hearts,
deserted poles with hollow burning middles.

In the unseen copulation,
in the waiting,
in manifestation.

Lost my locket

In the black hole that I am,
in the poetry of my earth, God can grow flowers.

I am the tunnel I went through where I totally lost it.
The costs of life seem meaningless to its unspeakable worth.

Looking for the treasure chest to save my locket
I went to flea markets across different countries.
Now help me to get rid of this thought:
I loved so much that I lost
before I could find it.

Wherever my hands found paint
I pressed them until black
on the inner bow of my ship.

Whoever finds my ribs write words on them please,
to tell nobody why I have been so addicted to words

In my dream I wear a locket with inside his picture.
His name only known by God,
only if there is one.

Nothing written but
the colour of his eyes.

With my children on a black bear

With a black bear as our mattress
and a blanket of night with planets
we watch when all things
that are dark move around us.

We remain silent, we are constantly,
we give light with each breath,
we are glow worms.
Along our light the lost
find their way back home.

Therefore, we are not afraid
even when darkness eats us
everything revolves around us

and round and round.

The both human both bear thing

Let us be,

both blue and dark-eyed,

both white furred, black haired,

both human, both bear,

in one coat with the universe

stitched on it. Embracing us in

one love, one star, one night.

The swan´s shen

Oh my Shen, I write it down the way it is
the words only a shadow of what I want to say.
A shadow of what is now bows over the paper,
circles around with holy smokes.

No one knows what caught the nest on fire
but it is burning on the water.
Mother-shen, mother swan hovers by with her little ones
Warms the water. Understands nothing,
gives the sky her rarely heard ga-oh.

The love of Shen has a beating heart
on the other side of the mirror.
The girl lays her cheek to the glass,
imitates the swans rarely heard
ga-oh.

I cry so I can love again.
Each and every one I see
I have to blow in Shen with
a rarely heard sound.
Now please,
cold water souls,
give me back my own.

Name my Shen when nothing is impossible.
Name sweet and I will find home.

When the night opens we sail away

Protected by the wide-winged owl we sail the unpredictable ocean
and while we cross in transformation a rainbow unfolds
in each of our ribcages.

The more we feel closed in by the waves,
the more we turn into a lighthouse for each other.

This way we shine to reach a flower not yet born.
Through a horn without wires we match with
our home. On its deep tone

the visionary looks straight into the night.
The shaman holds his drum so tight, to let
the loose rhythm of what goes on and on
flow through us.

The child sings about how much
he loves this voyage into his mother's kerchief
and the waves splash in the open mouth
of the moon's amazement.

Lips

I am opening up
the unmeasurable cold sky
slides inside
my whole face one smile
and I invite life daughter shaped

to dance her tiptoe on my roots
I kiss the empty sky
and you find your way
to my lips.

Birds

Our typewriting God
on paper of sky, ice-white
each typed black V, flies.

Tiny grasses dream

Tiny grasses dream about snow
The moon laying herself on them
weightless and cold
so their dreams grow
immaculately white
and wider.

Home is where the wasteland

Far from fragile minds in a bandage
far from their city in ruins of dreams
a tortoise white as sand white as tortoise
in its day in a skin crawling over skin.

Open bay for the sea to float in
the skyline it's prayer hums
the same deep sound as everything.

Free from the broken fragile minds
tearing open each other's bodies
with contrary dreams.

Will we ever be fulfilled while not being seen?
That close to darkness, the horizon holds the glow
of sunset.

Before it gets dark a mother
pours her love down into
her nameless future daughter.

Life pours her juice into new cells
for tomorrow's blooming.

Aztec lighthouse

Boy, my Aztec top is on.
I cut a sphinx out
to leave spaces.

There is no riddle in the answers
where it is impossible to fight, to dance
in the holes filled with light.

Boy fell asleep on the planet
with his belly full of waves,
wondering:

'Can those kids please stop
poking the jellyfishes on my beach?'
Everybody knows how kids fly high
on yelling 'No!'

Still there is no difference
between what I give light
and what I cut around.

Shoulder-blades white
contrast sharply
with night.

Wave, love

For L.

Wave when you see life's face, wave in your sophisticated way,
wave like you're educated, wave like you are on jazz,
wave like air is an instrument, wave at your past.

High on the tower, high on the sight, high above
the back of the deer, ride her with your eyes, sigh
over the world, sigh. Be the one who causes
the butterflies flight, the same blue as the sky
disappear to be here, go up in the height.

Blue on blue, live your truth.
No tears, no her, no me, no you.
Waterfall, granite, waterfall, granite.
The rhythm of a cuckoo cuckooing
over a nest with whose eggs?

Stop. A nest with no eggs.

Just walk until you fly
like you are melting into now
to be a wave, love.

The angel remains

Open your life today.

At first your eyes
and then, just to exercise,
your roof,
then the sky.

Fly to come down,
to open the earth.
Look at the hurt
with the intensity
of what you are worth.

Touch with all your senses,
open all the channels
just by saying yes
to flesh and soul.

Open it all
and see yourself waking up
in your own gentle hands.

No matter how wounded
the angel always remains.

Mammoth

When the sea came over the mammoth, did it cry?
When it lay flat on the bottom did its eye
still turn up, looking for the sky?

What my child means:
Did it mind? Does it matter? If the animal would have
been human would it have written a last letter?

Did the sea mean to take her? Is dying like falling asleep
or did she wake up? What was left when death peeled
off her mammoth-makeup? Is there something like
a break up?

Is it a loss or gain that we find these bones today
from what we did not know existed?

I dream a mammoth awake
to walk through my river.

Thus the whales fly

The Clean Northern-Wind And The Filthy Human Fingers

America

I want a pony to ride on at a tide that never changes
and a gun to protect us.

Star tells

There hangs a weather in the sky
chop down the white tree
he is too high, he touches a star
and we don't want to climb for real
we want to dream of climbing
and writing in the children's book
about the star and the tree
with in the middle where the white strings
binding it together, the fearful singing
of the threatening weather
that nears and nears
like something that nears forever
to touch the quiet tree who loves stars
to break down

So he is chopped
a hole to fill by human-hands with human-things (you don't need
hyphens here)
and the filthy human children
no longer make these things with
fingers but with machines

They make a ladder that reaches
and reaches.

Odyssey

Grown-up skinny, white men
who walk naked all together on moldy toes
through the park of a small city

They've got something on their heart
look with longing at the little golden bird
on the roof of the church
We are looking for a God, a sect or a woman
look at us, we surrender
(vomit runs red out of the mouth)

We are naked for you
if you can blow believe in my eyes

We are a water-balloon with purple veins

Save me
save me
save me

I am a poor, deadly simple man.

Concentration party

for the other who changed

I come to visit you I
wear a gasmask, everywhere
danger gasps, I stroke
the lice from your hair

Where have you been all that time

been working, you say
on a concentration party
also I've been a skinhead
everywhere I see concrete to
pee against, I have a logo and I spray
in thousand colours

You turn ever smaller
ever whiter
eyes earthy dim

My horse rears up
I eat you whole for antibodies.

Roleplay

(two farmers, a farmer's wife and a cow)

We have to find it
in the eyes of a
Clarabella

We already stare for a number of days
we will turn her over for this will possibly
twist everything

Take the hind legs, dear friend
you've grown, you deserved
to be able to turn over
something heavy

I will keep her calm
soften when you don't look
I will
stroke her head

The other farmer is afraid
of white, he pushes and lifts
only there where
the shadow patches are

Then it rains
then we make love in
the mud

And all the time change
roles.

Moult

A boy, her sick-bucket
a bed to sit on together
waiting until the unstoppable
flaming begins
A sentence he said
The way black can be pitch
so white is your skin

A window, through which she looks her eyes empty
this is what comes out: a jerk in a suit
the smog of the city, a blind cat
hair everywhere, trash, blowing over the water

The first thing she says:
I want to see and save what you
collected when you were nine

He sees her pictures of Victor and Rolf
strokes her back where his hand seems to live
and is still waiting for the flames.

Fox-heart

It is night, I skin a fox
to forget a few men
to at daytime be able to
eat fox heart from my blue lunchbox

That tastes like cherry with blood
that tastes like sweet of heart

Do you want to taste it
because it is also for seduction

That you like it
when the red drips down my chin
and leaves a wound in my white shirt
of lace.

Northern wind

The security men fall
a twisted chick shrieks
through the blue corridors

There the strip light claws
her eyes out, wants to bite soon
like, crab, cliff, clamber
Modern, modern, curved out of stone

Claws

There, the blood gets wrenched from
women's clothes in the wash-shed
nobody is allowed to know what I lisped
in the shadow of the red moon

There will come a woman with empty eyes
to ram and hit on the harp
there will stand a lioness,
a hater and a weasel
to grab the painting from your easel
to write words over it, over everything
those words that you do not want to hear
about what you've lost

But I sing:

In the back with that wind, in the back with that wind,

in the back with that wind.

Sistersserenades

Girl breathless

She is a girl without breath
but it doesn't matter
because she is in the thoughts
and the things
a butterfly
that I cannot find
but still, somewhere, somewhere
point or whisper
and I will believe it

If I am not mistaken
I can already hear from over there
(I point at air that seems more thin,
and soon will turn to pink)
her string orchestra
of every insect

so merry that it bleeds.

Dressing Up

You are a wafer-thin child
this way you've always been
does it have the colour if it
doesn't fit, did you get in
the kingfisher-suit (stand up, I'll do your hair)
scraped together (the mermaid throws up feathers)

'I am sorry I am a failure, gentleman
I am sorry about the endless silences
up the attic.'

Wings

I was at the children's party
of my sister
who was stillborn

She was here suddenly, like I had never missed her

Her little fingers fluttered
over my sun-face
it was a true winter
but terra, ochre, magenta sunlight

The girl's scattered paint-brushes
out of pure soft unicorn-hair
silver paint they scratched
with their little nails
from behind the bark
my sister's face strict
said ' do what I say!'

Paint a butterfly of me so I can fly again

I did so, I wanted her to stay
but knew well
an angel would never understand

And otherwise in the morning

I would have missed her way too much

If instead of flown off while waved goodbye

she would have been incomprehensibly erased.

Goodbye sister,

How beautiful you are
in your pink dress with peach pits

What is it like to lay on your belly
on a bed of clouds
to look down at us
how we bombard you
to a butterfly with sweet words

If you want it different I can
make an effort to learn to

Would you prefer to be a bat
or dental assistant
or ice queen

Show it to me through the shape of a cloud
I mean, you only have to say it

I allow everything
entirely.

Toothless

Truly, I found it
a disaster that I fell
a normal white-spotted plaster
on my abnormal blood-knee.
That night there passed
a crib-peddler by my nursery
to sell white squares
without a voice I yelled 'teeth?
I can hardly walk!'

I dreamed afterwards
that the girls next door flew

I stood on the ground

The following day everyone had teeth
in the mouth. 'I am incomplete' they said

They did nothing but biting.

Little collector

While I write there is a child who gathers
she carries a bag wherein the bones bump

She can't sleep they have told her
of chemicals in air and water, of all
that flies into your mouth while talking
that like this she may drown a spider

Anyway, all that stinks is dead or rotten
a blue or yellow body is broken

She only isn't afraid of bones
she collects them:
she rubs their white and clean, then silence.

This is a chest

Now she in her slow daily room,
stuffed with stone dogs and plants
has left the breathing for what it was:

Some kind of dragon to let go
without a chance to stare after because before
that time, with closed eyes, she falls into the earth

Mama earth ask her small fry questions
they hide in a white tissue and smell
that there somewhere far, no longer here
and snot makes no sense

The pen (where around there clasps a hand
attached to an arm
of a child)
who writes 'This' while she
wants it full of ever and life:

This, this, this.

The Heavy Beasts Rise, Sink

Seaclock

It breathes air, it's a mammal (Mr. Scruff)

Beautiful mammal that I am
heavy body that lives around me

Time eats it empty
there are cold spoons for that

First feed the little mouth
that snaps, don't leave it
in the dark even little fish
look for words
nipples
names

Forgetting will be like sleeping

The sea, I know her
longer than today

She will make us sail, wave, wave, bear.

Blue jay

The blue jay calls
in all tonalities in the lower lands
the falling of the light and night begins

In valleys I stay hidden
in folds still whimsical
for stillness
to want is now forbidden

with raw umber
I colour the weather
natural.

Seamusic

Flying whales
above me, I only smell
the sweet bones, think
about your salt of sea

And where are the boys
where the marching men
with their glimmering black boots

Who comes to command me
ask no questions anymore

And carries me to the boat
that arrives with silences
and Chinese blossoms.

White fan

(each fold reels out sadness)

1.

The death moan
'we just don't get off-ill'
who thought this out
nightmares reach
with tails into dreams.

2.

Hitting like a dragon
doesn't give complacency

I don't want to
give me the kite
the white, tender
apple.

3.

Followers, the
following: 'everything
is over now
lay your egg on
the middle of the earth

who dies the quickest
suffers least.'

4.
It seems to you beautiful
and horrible at the same time
the girl bites with
shark teeth
bat's head
from body.

5.
Long slim hair
blond round ass
my rounds around
and cherry mouth
touch me, I
am a woman
to bathe in.

6.
Pulling out each other's feet again
underneath the oil lamp light
where we alternately sear a wing

The game who can get

the closest to the fire-giving flower

to glow but not to die: that is our opium.

7.

Did you blame the crab

for having scissors

Such an oddity

wouldn't he preferably

ask another to carry

his lancinating shell

Sings the queen

Even the bittersweet swans

stretch their necks and quack

for him.

8.

I am having a characterless Sunday

I shine absolutely nothing

and that will do

today my face is called

visage

you're the scoop in my sand
that leaves no traces

I am the unconquered
crow princess in love and
six, I enjoy your hopeless
floundering in the water.

Firesea

Where I can't get away from
lava glows towards me

The building is of course
big, from glass

With knees that cannot dance

The captain I will kill
a blue thread that
draws itself tight
when he falls

Reasons:

1. His fish-stick heart, looks fabulous
with the navy blue of his suit
it is a scream

2. After all, the being controlled
runs way past bearing
streaming from stormy streams

3. One can't live in voices

that steam up all windows

The lavagirl experiences this differently

lava only gives her the pimples.

Picture

The castle is the wide
range of pain
in the biggest room
I am on a gala
in a dress
that doesn't fit

The lackey is a dick
smacking his lips eating porridge
wears a dark brown suit
can further be recognized by
a wet, sad smell

How baby stars...

He admires my dress
'Amazing!'

in her cracks, he urges things
until the seams tear in long threads

How baby stars shine in the sky

A paper tent and then ragging

with those needles

The girl over there in the dress that tears

I turn it into a 'find the picture.'

Amber

As squid-beaks turn into amber
in sperm whales' intestines
what does my death-cry
do with you when you eat me?

Will I leave a sign that eats back at you?
Hieroglyphs squid black until the end of time.

Or will it ask you to forget me here at the sea
to let it blow away.

About the Author

Laura Demelza Bosma (1986) is a mother of three, artist, poetess and translator. She has been active as a poetess in the Netherlands, winning poetryslams and writing prices for youth. Her work appeared in various anthologies and in 2007 in her poetry chapbook 'Zo vliegen de walvissen' (Thus the whales fly). She studied and graduated in Writing For Performance at the HKU, the art-academy in Utrecht.

www.laurademelzabosma.com

www.ingramcontent.com/pod-product-compliance
Lightning Source LLC
LaVergne TN
LVHW091154080426
835509LV00006B/679